POLICE DOGS

by Frances E. Ruffin

Consultant: Wilma Melville, Founder
National Disaster Search Dog Foundation

BEARPORT
PUBLISHING COMPANY, INC.

New York, New York

Special thanks to Wilma Melville who founded the:
National Disaster Search Dog Foundation
206 N. Signal Street, Suite R
Ojai, CA 93023
(888) 4K9-HERO
www.SearchDogFoundation.org

The Search Dog Foundation is a not-for-profit organization that rescues dogs, gives them professional training, and partners them with firefighters to find people buried alive in disasters. They produce the most highly trained search dogs in the nation.

To David Woods,
who served as a military police officer
in the United States Air Force

Design and production by Dawn Beard Creative and Octavo Design and Production, Inc.

Credits

Cover, Front(left), AP / Wide World Photos, (top right), Reuters / CORBIS; (center right), AP / Wide World Photos; (bottom right), courtesy, Deputy Jim Bauerly, Woodbury County, Iowa Sheriff's Department; Back (top), Reuters / CORBIS; (center), AP / Wide World Photos, (bottom), courtesy, Deputy Jim Bauerly, Woodbury County, Iowa Sheriff's Department. Title page, AP / Wide World Photos. Page 3, Reuters / CORBIS; 4-5, Corbis / Fotosearch; 4, courtesy, Deputy Jim Bauerly, Woodbury County, Iowa Sheriff's Department; 6-7, David R. Frazier Photolibrary; 7, AP / Wide World Photos; 8-9, Viesti Associates; 9, Index Stock / Fotosearch; 10-11, Library of Congress Prints & Photographs Collection; 11, Swim Ink / CORBIS; 12-13, CORBIS; 14-15, Dale C. Spartas / CORBIS; 15, Reuters / CORBIS; 16-17, Dennis Light / Light Photographic; 17, Bob Eden / Eden Consulting Group; 18, AP / Wide World Photos; 18-19, Robert Llewellyn / CORBIS; 20-21(both), AP / Wide World Photos; 22-23, William Mullins; 23, Turnley / SIPA; 24, The Herald, Everett, Washington; 25, Stacey Hillman / Pennies to Protect Police Dogs; 26-27, Tom Nebbia / CORBIS; 29(top left), Yann Arthus-Bertrand / CORBIS; 29(top center), Photodisc / Fotosearch; 29(top right), Photospin.com; 29(center), Photodisc / Fotosearch; 29(bottom right), John Daniels / Ardea; 29(bottom left), Tim Davis / Photo Researchers, Inc.

Library of Congress Cataloging-in-Publication Data

Ruffin, Frances E.
  Police dogs / by Frances E. Ruffin; consultant, Wilma Melville.
    p. cm.—(Dog heroes)
  Includes bibliographical references and index.
  ISBN 1-59716-014-8 (lib. bdg.)   ISBN 1-59716-037-7 (pbk.)
  1. Police dogs—Juvenile literature. I. Melville, Wilma. II. Title. III. Series

HV8025.R84 2005
363.2'32—dc22

                        2004020752

For more information, write to Bearport Publishing Company, Inc., 101 Fifth Avenue, Suite 6R, New York, New York 10003. Printed in the United States of America.

1 2 3 4 5 6 7 8 9 10

Table of Contents

A Nighttime Chase

In the dark streets, the car thief thought he could get away from the police. When it seemed safe, he pulled over the stolen car and jumped out. Minutes after he ran into the woods, however, the police found the car. Right away, the officers knew they'd need help to search the woods.

Officer Jim Bauerly and his dog, Sipo, were called. At first, Sipo ran back and forth through the woods, his nose in the air. Then he smelled something and gave a bark. When Jim caught up to him, Sipo was holding on to the thief's arm!

Officer Jim Bauerly and Sipo

Depending on the weather and the site, a bloodhound can follow a person's smell even if it's 10 days old.

Dog Detectives

Dogs are important members of police departments around the world. Why do police officers need their help? Dogs are born **detectives**. They hear and smell things much better than a person. A police dog can learn to smell even a small amount of a drug.

A police dog sniffs for drugs at the Mexican border.

Dogs can see the smallest movement from far away. They can also run much faster than a person. If a **suspect** runs away from a crime scene, a police dog can often catch him. These skills help make dogs powerful crime fighters.

Gator and his partner, Police Officer Neil Gang, search Surprise Stadium in Arizona.

Dogs can see a mouse moving from 100 yards away.

The K-9 Team

Every police dog has one human **partner**, or **handler**. Together, the dog and handler are called a K-9 team. "K-9" is another way of writing "canine," which means "dog." A police dog's first **duty** is to protect his partner. Officers say their dogs would die to protect them.

Police dogs are trained to grab a suspect's arm and hold on, but not bite. The dog won't let go until his partner comes with handcuffs.

Most police dogs are large and look frightening. Sometimes just seeing a police dog can make a person stay still.

Some police dogs have jaws so strong they could break a person's arm.

Police Dog History

Dogs have helped hunt down **criminals** for more than 500 years. By 1770, the town of St. Malo in France, a country in Europe, had a police dog program. In the late 1800s, police dogs were common in Belgium and Germany, two countries also in Europe.

Almost 100 years ago, police departments in the United States began using dogs. These animals were often used to track down people who had escaped from prison.

The best tracking dogs are bloodhounds. Their noses are more powerful than most other dogs. Two bloodhounds once trailed a stolen horse 135 miles across Kansas.

French police dogs in action in 1905

In the United States, bloodhounds were used to track enemy soldiers as far back as 1841.

Police dogs helping control crowds in 1905

K-9's Finest

Several **breeds** of dog are best for police work. Most police departments around the world use German shepherds. These large dogs are smart and friendly. They have strong, powerful bodies and can be very forceful when the job calls for it.

The German word for German shepherd is "Polizeihund." This word means "police dog."

Doberman pinschers are also popular police K-9s. They are tall and lean. These dogs look **fierce** and are very **protective** of their handlers.

Other big breeds that become part of police K-9 teams are Belgian Malinois, rottweilers, bloodhounds, and Labrador retrievers. Retrievers are good at sniffing out drugs and weapons.

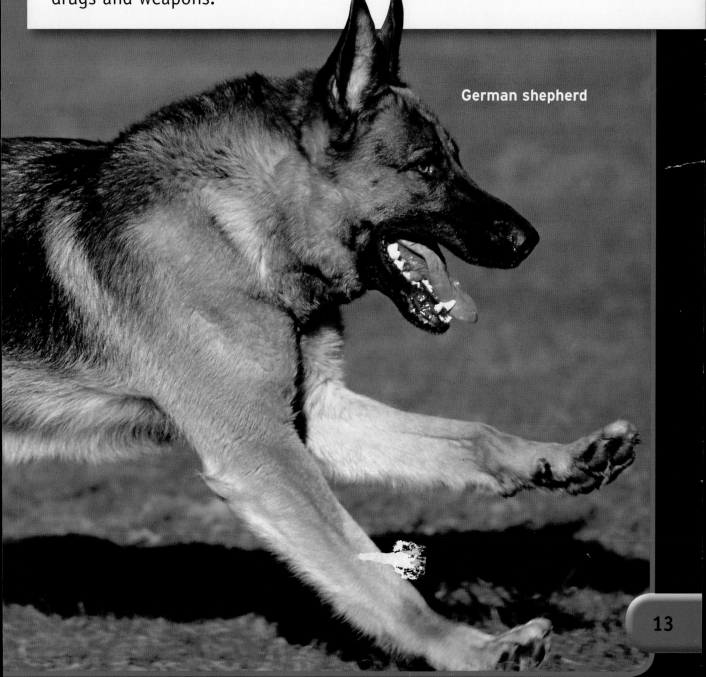

German shepherd

Puppy Tests

Trainers test puppies to see if they will make good police dogs. The animals must enjoy learning. They need to be smart, friendly, and curious.

In one test, the trainer jangles keys. If the puppy moves toward them, he shows that he's curious about what made the noise. He may become a good detective.

In another test, a puppy is put on different kinds of floors. One floor is slippery. Another is rough. How does he react? If he can't **adjust** to new things, then he won't make a good police dog.

Once a puppy becomes a police dog, he often gets to wear a bulletproof vest. Here, Cim and his handler Doug show off Cim's vest.

A puppy is also tested to see if he can be trained easily. He is held on his back. At first, he will struggle. If he quickly relaxes, he will probably have no trouble learning.

The Training Begins

By the age of two, police dogs are paired with their human partners. Together, they attend K-9 training school.

Police dogs must be strong and quick. In school, they learn to jump through open car windows. They are taught to climb walls that are six feet high. They crawl through tunnels and leap up on piles of barrels.

Dogs in training sometimes go with their partners to the firing range. The officers practice shooting guns. The dogs must get used to the sound. On the job, they have to stay calm, no matter how noisy it is.

Some dogs don't finish police dog training because they are too active or easily frightened.

Searching for Drugs

Training a police dog to search for drugs can seem like play at first. The handler and the dog start a game of tug of war with a towel. The dog likes this game.

A dog learning how to search at a training center in Maryland

A police dog named Zekuno could smell a very small amount of a drug, even if it was hidden in the seat cushion of a car.

Then the handler puts a drug inside the towel and hides it. The dog uses his strong sense of smell to find the towel. He is then rewarded with another game of tug of war. After some practice, the dog learns to find the drug without the towel.

A Nose for Trouble

Most police dogs are trained to sniff out drugs. They can also sniff out people. Every person has a different **scent**. Dogs can tell these scents apart. They can follow a person's scent anywhere.

A bloodhound named Buddy and his handler search a forest for a suspect.

A dog's sense of smell is 1,000 times better than a person's sense of smell.

Dogs can sometimes chase the scent of a person driving a car. Some of the person's scent drifts out of the car. A dog in New York once tracked a suspect for three miles along the highway.

A police dog's **identification** of a person by scent is very **reliable**. It can be used as **evidence** in court.

Patrolling the Streets

A police dog **patrols** with his partner day and night. The dog is calm and friendly. He's always ready for action.

Sometimes when an officer pulls over a speeding car, the driver gets angry. While the officer writes a ticket, his dog hangs out of the car window, barking. This action sends a message to the driver to stay calm.

If a **burglar** alarm goes off, a K-9 team is sometimes called. At first, the police dog enters the building alone. He will grab anyone hiding inside. Then the officer can safely go into the building and arrest the burglar.

A police dog watches a suspect get arrested at the 1998 World Cup Soccer match in France.

Always ask for the police officer's permission before petting his or her dog.

Danger on the Job

Police work is dangerous. Like their human partners, dogs sometimes get hurt.

Ikon, an eight-year-old German shepherd, had caught 80 suspects in his life. In 2003, he chased a man selling drugs. The man ran across a freeway. Ikon followed him and was struck by a car and killed.

Hundreds of people went to this memorial service, where Officer Chip Higinbotham spoke about Ikon's life and work.

Officer Loyal Higinbotham & K-9 Ikon

Other police dogs have been shot by criminals. In 2001, 10-year-old Stacey Hillman of Florida read a story about the dangers police dogs face. She decided to help the dogs get bulletproof vests. Stacey has raised more than $120,000. She wants every police dog in Florida to have a vest.

Deputy Sheriff Ramos, Brutus, and Stacey Hillman

A Partner and a Pet

Most police dogs live with their handlers. The team is together 24 hours a day, seven days a week. Police dogs protect their partners. Together, the K-9 team protects the public.

Police dogs are faithful and fearless members of police departments. They are ready to give their lives in the line of duty. After many long years of service, most dogs **retire** to the comfort of their handlers' backyard. Their good work, however, is never forgotten.

Police dogs don't stop training until they retire.

Just the Facts

- Bloodhounds were once the only breed of dog that could give evidence in court. Today, other breeds can also give evidence.

- A burglar once broke into a building by breaking a window with a rock he had picked up out of the mud. A bloodhound found the burglar's scent in the holes his fingers made in the mud. The burglar was soon caught.

- Dogs can smell fear. When people are afraid, they give off a strong scent. This scent makes it even easier for dogs to trail someone running away from the police.

- Some police dogs are trained to sniff for bombs. If a dog finds one, he alerts his handler by sitting next to it. Scratching at the bomb might make it explode.

- Police dogs are almost always male. Male dogs are larger and weigh more than females, which makes it easier for them to protect their handlers.

- Many American police departments get their dogs from European countries. Some of these dogs never learn to obey **commands** in English. They only understand commands in the first language they learned.

Common Breeds: POLICE DOGS

Belgian Malinois

German shepherd

Doberman pinscher

Labrador retriever

bloodhound

rottweiler

adjust (uh-JUHST) to get used to something new

breeds (BREEDZ) types of a certain animal

burglar (BURG-lur) someone who breaks into a building in order to steal things

commands (kuh-MANDZ) instructions given to be obeyed; orders

criminals (KRIM-uh-nuhlz) people who commit a crime, or something against the law

detectives (di-TEK-tivz) people who solve crimes

duty (DOO-tee) something a person must do or should do

evidence (EV-uh-duhnss) information and facts that help give proof of something

fierce (FIHRSS) wild and dangerous

handler (HAND-lur) someone who trains and works with animals

identification (*eye*-den-tuh-fuh-KAY-shuhn) the act of recognizing or showing who someone is

partner (PART-nur) one of two or more people or animals who do something together

patrols (puh-TROHLZ) walks around an area in order to guard it

protective (pruh-TEK-tiv) keeping something safe from danger

reliable (ri-LYE-uh-buhl) able to be trusted and depended on

retire (ri-TIRE) to stop working, usually because of age

scent (SENT) the smell of a person or animal

suspect (SUHSS-pekt) someone thought to have committed a crime

Bibliography

Bidner, Jen. *Dog Heroes: Saving Lives and Protecting America.* Guilford, CT: Lyons Press (2002).

Farran, Christopher. *Dogs on the Job! True Stories of Phenomenal Dogs.* New York, NY: Avon (2001).

Jackson, Donna M. *Hero Dogs: Courageous Canines in Action.* New York, NY: Little, Brown and Company (2003).

Owens, Carrie. *Working Dogs.* Rocklin, CA: Prima Publishing (1999).

Singer, Marilyn. *A Dog's Gotta Do What a Dog's Gotta Do.* New York, NY: Henry Holt and Company (2000).

Steiger, Brad, and Sherry Hansen Steiger. *Dog Miracles: Inspirational and Heroic True Stories.* Holbrook, MA: Adams Media (2001).

Weisbord, Merrily, and Kim Kachanoff. *Dogs with Jobs: Working Dogs around the World.* New York, NY: Pocket Books (2000).

Read More

Needles, Colleen, and Kit Carlson. *Working Dogs: Tales from Animal Planet's K-9 to 5 World.* New York, NY: Discovery Books (2000).

Rathman, Peggy. *Officer Buckle and Gloria.* New York, NY: Putnam (1995).

Russell, Joan Plummer, and Kris Turner Sinnenberg. *Aero and Officer Mike: Police Partners.* Honesdale, PA: Boyds Mills (2001).

Learn More Online

Visit these Web sites to learn more about police dogs:

http://dogswithjobs.com/about_dogs/about.htm

http://people.howstuffworks.com/police-dog.htm

http://policedogfoundation.org/html/fun_facts.html

Index

About the Author

Frances E. Ruffin has written many nonfiction books for children. She lives and writes in New York City.